This
David Bennett Book
belongs to

_____

_____

_____

_____

To Tom, Tom, Joe,
Caroline & Tom

First published in paperback in 1993
by David Bennett Books Ltd,
94 Victoria Street, St Albans,
Herts, AL1 3TG.
First published in hardback in 1991
by Kingfisher Books

BRITISH LIBRARY CATALOGUING IN PUBLICATION DATA
A catalogue record for this book is available
from the British Library.
ISBN 1 85602 041 X

Typesetting by Type City
Production by Imago
Printed in Hong Kong

The Monster Book of A·B·C Sounds
by
Alan Snow

David Bennett Books

The hide and seek game
is about to begin.

Aa

The door is ajar
and the rats go right in.
(This monster wasn't quite ready.)

Bb

A monster pops out
from behind a small door,

Cc

while three cunning rats
sneak a look 'neath the floor.

Dd

Some rats sniff about and
look all round the clock.

Ee

Two more go upstairs and are in for a shock.

Ff

While one monster slips
in the chase and gets wet...

Hh

This ticklish young monster
is found by his feet.

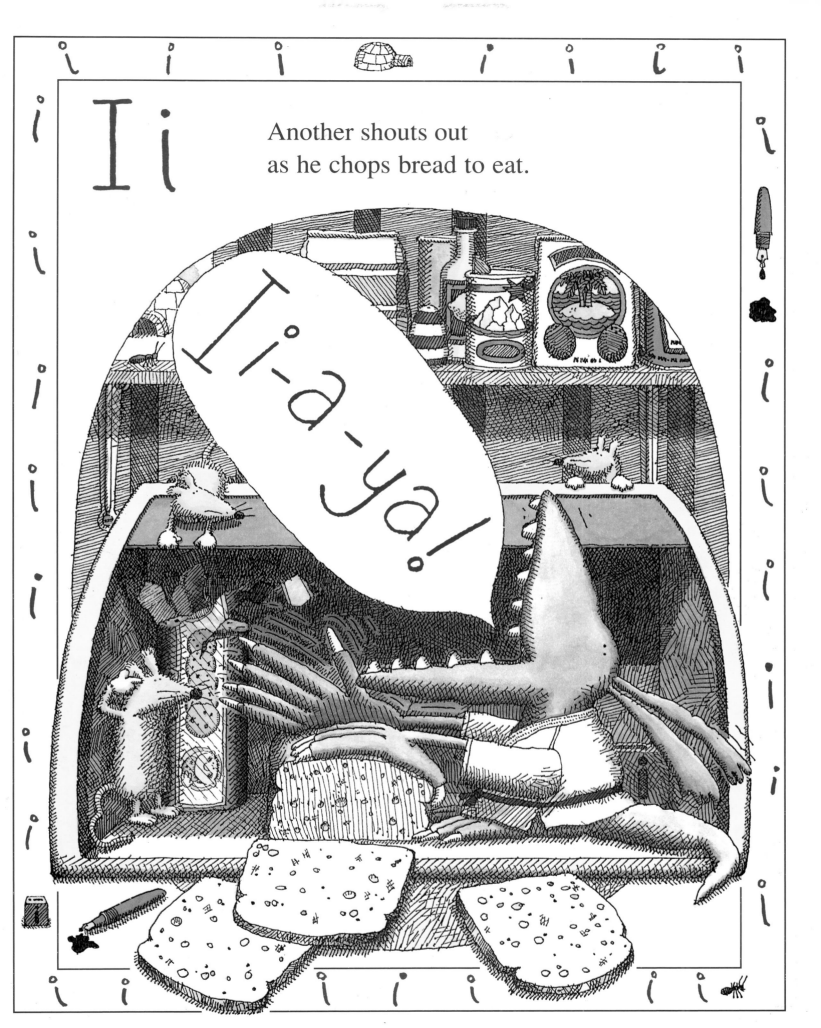

Mm

and this one finds honey,
which doesn't last long.

Nn

A very bold monster
knocks rats out for six.

Oo

He flies upside down
and does other brave tricks.

OoOoooh!

P p

Oops! This little monster runs right out of luck...

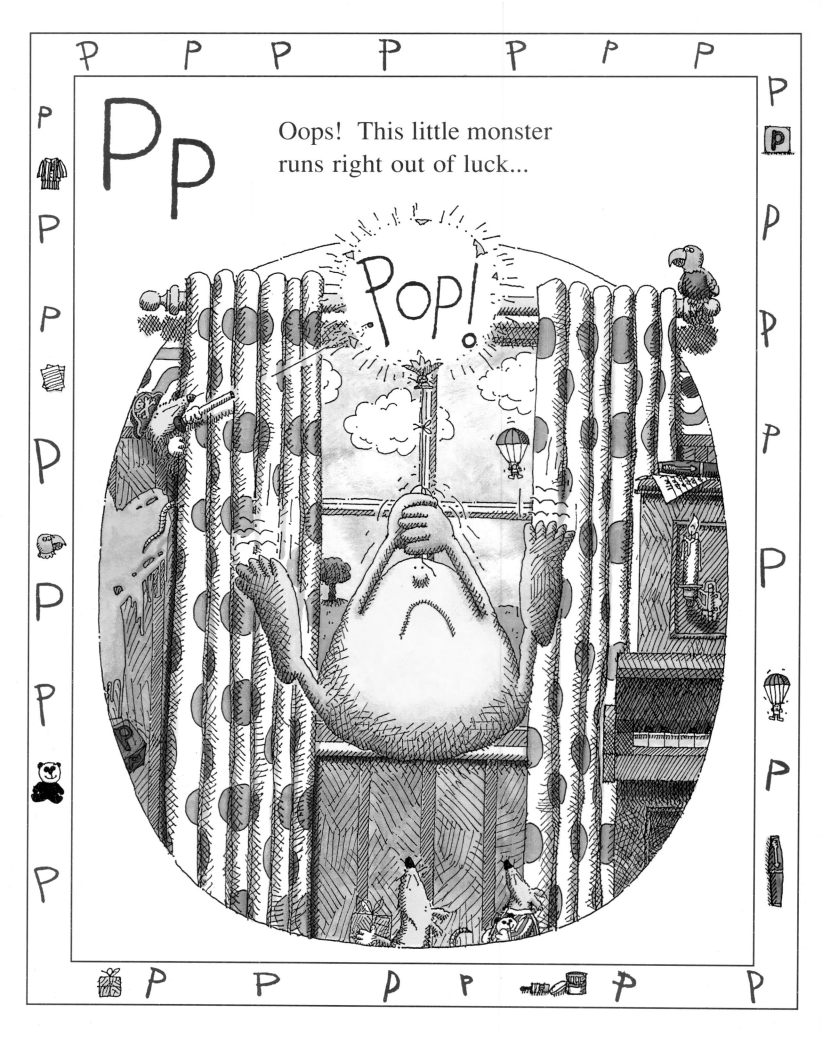

Rr

The hairiest monster
is big, bad and mean.

Ss

A slithery monster hopes
not to be seen.

Tt

This monster is gasping
with hunger and thirst.

Uu

He goes to the cupboard,
but rats got there first.

V v

"I bet you can't catch me!"
is this monster's boast.

Ww

"That's easy," the rat laughs.
"You're last past the post!"

Wheeeeee

They all cuddle up in their warm, cosy bed,
and dream of their monster hunt -
A through to Z.

The End.

Other David Bennett paperbacks you will enjoy . . .

I am a Duck *Linda Bygrave • Louise Voce*   *ISBN 1 85602 054 1*

I am a Frog *Linda Bygrave • Louise Voce*   *ISBN 1 85602 051 7*

I am a Butterfly *Linda Bygrave • Louise Voce*   *ISBN 1 85602 052 5*

I am a Rabbit *Linda Bygrave • Louise Voce*   *ISBN 1 85602 053 3*

As featured on BBC TV's *Playdays*. The perfect nature library for the very young.

If Dinosaurs Came To Town *Dom Mansell*   *ISBN 1 85602 044 4*

'. . . combines detailed pictures and evocative language with inviting tit-bits of science' *The Independent*

The Monster Book of ABC Sounds *Alan Snow*   *ISBN 1 85602 041 X*

An ABC of sounds, which follows a riotous game of hide-and-seek between a group of rats and monsters.

Inside Big Machines *Arlene Blanchard • Tony Wells*   *ISBN 1 85602 043 6*

A fascinating look inside some of the world's biggest machines.

Teddy Bear, Teddy Bear *Carol Lawson*   *ISBN 1 85602 040 1*

A beautifully illustrated version of the classic children's activity rhyme.

One Cow Moo Moo! *David Bennett • Andy Cooke*   *ISBN 1 85602 042 8*

As featured on BBC TV's *Over The Moon*. A farmyard romp through numbers from one to ten.

Coming soon from David Bennett paperbacks

The Christmas Party *Julie Lacome*   *ISBN 1 85602 068 1*

A story book and activity book rolled into one, full of festive ideas to keep kids busy!

Our Home and Garden Catalogue *Joanne Flindall*   *ISBN 1 85602 069 X*

A wonderful word book for the very young, packed with over 1000 items which can be found around the home.

The Secrets of Santa *Annie Civardi • Clive Scruton*   *ISBN 1 85602 070 3*

Peregrine Penguin, chief reporter for the South Polar Times, records Santa's preparations for Christmas.